THE PARAPROFESSIONALS
OR
TEACHER AIDES

THE PARAPROFESSIONALS
or
TEACHER AIDES

SELECTION, PREPARATION AND ASSIGNMENT

Paul C. Shank
and
Wayne McElroy

PENDELL
PUBLISHING
COMPANY

Library of Congress Catalog Card Number; 70-107603

TO
our wives

Yvonne Shank and Sue McElroy

CONTENTS

PREFACE

The authors of this handbook have had experience with teacher aides at each level of concern: the teacher with an aide; the school principal, in whose building aides have worked; the district superintendent, responsible for providing relevant information necessary to policy formulation by the board of education, and responsible for employing teacher aides; and as professors of education responsible for developing training programs for teacher aides.

The Purposes

The purposes of this handbook are therefore three-fold. First, to provide teachers and school administrators with a guide for the selection, preparation and assignment of teacher aides. Second, to set forth some practical information for teacher aides. Third, to present lessons of proven worth and three methods of organization for the teaching of these lessons. Instructional programs for teacher aides may be offered by personnel within the school district, a college, an adult education program or in a two-year college terminal program.

Teacher Aide Defined

The term *teacher aide* as used in this handbook is: those non-certified (teacher certification) personnel who directly aid the teacher and/or work with pupils under the supervision of the teacher. Many schools employ persons fitting this definition, but refer to them as para-professionals, volunteers, teacher helpers or sub-professionals. There are nearly as many descriptive terms for teacher aides as discussed here, as there are school districts in which they are employed.

This Handbook: Its Uses and Users

The practical benefits and usage of this handbook are closely related to the purposes outlined above. It is suggested that it serve administrators as they assist the board of education in the formulation of policies relative to teacher aides. Further, that criteria for selection and sample application forms will prove useful to administrators charged with the responsibility for hiring teacher aides.

The selection dealing with teacher - teacher aide relationships will be of interest to teachers, and college students enrolled in teacher preparation programs. Teachers may gain insights into the wide variety of tasks within the capabilities of teacher aides, and how they can use these capabilities to maximize instruction of pupils.

There is much of value in this handbook for teacher aides. A general concept of the role of the teacher aide and how it relates to other school personnel will benefit new teacher aides and those contemplating this service. Of special usefulness are the descriptions of specific tasks and opportunities for preparation for these tasks.

Institutions, including two-year and four-year colleges, responsible for training programs for teacher aides should reap a bountiful harvest from the lesson outlines included in this handbook. Each lesson presented has been used with success in programs developed to train or re-train teacher aides. Presently the preparation of teacher aides is primarily the responsibility of the school district in which they work. Most school districts find it expedient to "farm out" this responsibility for preparation of teacher aides. The advantage of well prepared teacher aides accrues primarily to the school district in which they work: to the pupils, teachers, and teacher aides.

ACKNOWLEDGMENTS

No statement of purpose regarding a recent development in education can effectively be set forth without the contributions of many interested professionals. The authors wish to express their appreciation to several persons who assisted in the development and evaluation of some of the lessons included in this book. Dr. Kenneth Tillman, physical education; Dr. Paul E. Mawhinney, education; Mrs. Janet Watkins, registered nurse; Mrs. Yvonne Shank, professional social worker; and Dr. Kenneth S. Moxey, psychology. To the many others who offered suggestions and criticisms, we say thanks.

CHAPTER I
INTRODUCTION

As teaching has become more specialized, the preparation period length-ened, and technical support devices developed, it is logical that a cadre of assistants and specialists be employed to aide the teacher. Skilled tradesmen and professionals alike have helpers or technicians to support them as they ply their trade or practice their profession. The mason, with the support of a hod carrier, laborers, and an apprentice is responsible for a craftsman-like job. The dentist, with the support of a dental technician, receptionist, X-ray tech-nician, and craftsmen who make replicas of original teeth, can devote his full energy and skill to treating the particular dental problem of the patient.

The practice of using teacher aides in school systems has grown rapidly in the past decade and is still accelerating. This trend will continue as the pres-sures of new knowledge and an ever increasing number of pupils force schools to seek maximum service from fully prepared and certified teachers.

The Administrative Responsibility

Most school systems include teacher aides in their policy statement re-garding non-professional or non-certified staff. It would be wise that three statements be included in this section of the school policy relevant to teacher aides. A separate statement setting the guidelines for: 1) selection of teacher aides, 2) preparation programs for teacher aides, and 3) the assignment of teacher aides. As will be discussed at some length in succeeding chapters herein, these policy statements should be broad reflections of the particular needs and philosophy of the school district on which administrative practices and procedures can be based.

1

INTRODUCTION

It is the administration's responsibility to develop a selection criteria, including information about applicants, to serve as a basis for the employment of aides. This must be accomplished within the framework of the board of education policy referred to above.

The responsibility for preparation programs and/or in-service training of teacher aides also falls to the administrative personnel. Options for meeting this responsibility are discussed in a later chapter.

The assignment of teacher aides will necessarily be based upon teacher requests, the number of aides available and the skills they possess. The assignment and supervision of teacher aides is usually the task of the building administrator, normally the principal.

As a basis for administrative practice in the fulfillment of the responsibilities relevant to teacher aides the following suggestions are offered:

1. Review policies relating to teacher aides annually.

2. Allow appropriate flexibility in administrative practices and procedures pertaining to teacher aides.

3. Provide for an annual evaluation of teacher aide enhancement of the instructional program; including efficient use of aides by teachers.

4. Provide for annual evaluation of individual teacher aide task performance.

5. Seek suggestions for improved use of teacher aides from teachers and aides. Use these suggestions in the revision of policies, practices and procedures relating to teacher aides.

6. Strive for an administrative structure based on the premise that it is the *teacher* who is being aided, and instruction of pupils is the *task* with which the teacher is being aided.

The Teacher and the Aide

Fundamental to efficient use of teacher aides is a cordial relationship between the teacher and the aide serving with her. An understanding of their separate and coordinated roles is of prime import to this relationship. Teachers

2

must be appraised of all relevant information about aides before the aides are assigned. The guideline in federally funded programs for training of teacher aides specify a certain portion of the training program must include teachers and teacher aides learning together. Teachers should have a voice in these assignments of teacher aides, especially if an aide is to work closely with one certain teacher. The following list is suggested for teachers to whom aides are assigned.

1. Be sure your directions are clear, and the aide understands what is expected of her.

2. Be patient with and respectful of the aide.

3. Remember — aides serve to help you improve instruction, and to allow you an opportunity for additional individualized instruction.

4. Be willing to teach the aide skills she can learn and wants to learn. Include the reasons for the task as well as the "how to" information.

5. When corrections or reprimands are necessary — make them in private: never in the presence of pupils. Also, an attitude of improving the instructional climate for pupils should prevail in such cases.

Teachers should understand their responsibility for evaluating the contribution of the teacher aide in terms of their own improved teaching. This should be an on-going evaluation carried on with the full knowledge and cooperation of the aide, and resulting in a semi-annual report.

The Teacher Aide

In order to make a maximum contribution to the education of children the teacher aide must know where she fits into the educational process, what is the focus of her job and how she can grow and improve in her position. Two concepts most important to a positive attitude on the part of teacher aides are: 1) aides serve teachers, either directly or indirectly, that more attention may be given pupils, and 2) growth in her job is dependent on attention and effort at school and participation in educational programs designed to teach the aide how to perform present tasks better and to perform new tasks.

Optimum service by teacher aides is also dependent upon establishing positive relationships with teachers, children and other school staff members. The teacher aide must view her job as important work worth doing, without overstepping her position or being critical of others striving to facilitate learning. This list of suggestions to help teacher aides maintain positive relationships with other school personnel and to pursue her tasks with enthusiasm are appropriate.

1. Be patient, and respectful of teachers with whom you work. Remember, they are learning to use your services as you are learning to serve.

2. Any task necessary to promote learning by pupils is worthy of performance with pride and diligence.

3. Teachers are teaching because they are dedicated to their profession, but being human, they too make mistakes.

4. If you have questions regarding a task you are asked to perform, ask. Try to understand thoroughly what is expected of you.

5. Give the school administration your loyal support, the teachers your best assistance and the pupils your best nature.

6. Resolve to seek new information and to develop new skills that will enable you to be of greater assistance each school year. The pupils aren't the only people in school who should be learning.

Summary

The continued growth in numbers of teacher aides employed in schools attests to the worth of this relatively new venture by American schools. The future may well find teacher aides as indispensable in schools as are nurse aides in hospitals. There may well be evolved one and two year preparation programs for teacher aides. The authors believe this trend will develop as a substantial terminal program in the two-year colleges. Hopefully, there will be no prerequisites other than normal health and interest, and the offerings of such a program will be geared to the aide rather than patterned after existing teacher education programs. Some teacher aides may profit by six weeks of intensive technical training, while others may find a year or more of semi-academic study of more value.

In schools where teacher aides have served successfully for several years, programs of in-service education have been a significant factor. Well defined roles and role-relationships for teachers and teacher aides are also the rule. Further, continual evaluation and re-evaluation of teacher aide programs have been reflected in policy revisions and changing administrative practices and procedures.

CHAPTER II

SELECTION OF TEACHER AIDES

Basic to the selection of personnel for service in any institution is the need for the performance of meaningful tasks by those persons to be selected. The more clearly the tasks can be defined in terms of hours, skills, human interaction and desired productive endeavor, the more exacting can be the qualifications expected of those seeking acceptance. Thus, the school planning to initiate, expand or maintain the practice of using teacher aides must first determine: 1) What are their needs?, 2) How will the school organization incorporate teacher aides into the education program?, and 3) Who is available for this service?

Determining Needs

Needs should be determined cooperatively by teachers and the building administrators. The teachers' responsibility is primarily that of justification of need. This will require delineation of specific tasks to be performed, the time required, and the skills necessary for satisfactory task performance. The principal's responsibility is planning for proper supervision and appropriate evaluation of the services of teacher aides. He will need the full cooperation of teachers to adequately plan and perform these two functions. They are, however, his responsibility.

After the needs for teacher aides have been determined for each building, the building administrators (principals) should confer with the district supervisor charged with hiring non-certified personnel and/or the superintendent of schools. At this conference plans for the use of teacher aides, their supervision and evaluation procedures can be discussed prior to reaching a decision regarding the number and type of teacher aides to be employed.

SELECTION OF TEACHER AIDES

Tasks Aides Can Perform

The number of tasks teacher aides can perform is infinite. This variety of tasks to be performed is an appealing attraction to those persons serving as teacher aides. The range of skills needed to perform the varied tasks is nearly as extensive as the background of personal and work experience characteristics of those seeking to become teacher aides.

The many tasks fall into two broad categories: those tasks in which the aide has contact with students, and those tasks that are primarily clerical, service oriented, or technical. Essentially, the teacher aides may be assigned to work directly with students, or to work in a supporting role removed from direct contact with students. As would be expected some tasks are a combination of these two categorical descriptions.

Table I, is a listing of tasks normally performed by teacher aides in schools. Each task is designated as being in one of the two categories described above. It is to be noted that specific chores are included, many of which are similar. This will prod the imagination of the reader. It would be naive to assume all possible tasks or combinations of tasks are included.

TABLE I

SPECIFIC TASKS AND THEIR PRIMARY ORIENTATION

Tasks	Student Contact	Supportive Role	Both
Supervise recess	x		
Prepare flash cards	x		
Help with independent reading	x		
Distribute materials			x
Give safety tests	x		
Prepare and install decorations			x
Get children ready for meals	x		
Prepare for and supervise rest periods	x		
Play with small groups	x		
Help teachers with clerical work		x	x
Tell stories or read to pupils	x		
Make costumes		x	x
Chaperone activities	x		
Conduct money raising projects		x	x

TABLE I (Continued)

Tasks	Student Contact	Supportive Role	Both
Supervise eating areas	x		
Make and repair toys for primary children		x	
Typing and duplicating instructional materials		x	
Tape record stories		x	
Supervise after-school study rooms	x		
Compile and maintain files of pictures, stories and articles for independent study		x	
Supervise clean-up chores	x		
Teach nursery rhymes	x		
Operate filmstrip projectors, 16mm projectors, recorders, and individual viewers			x
Help organize games			x
Set up machines designed for individual work		x	
Help students learn to use machines designed for individualized instruction	x		
Help children use toys, game or play equipment	x		
Tutor individual students	x		
Assist teachers on field trips			x
Gather materials from outside sources		x	
Help with checking pupils' work			x
Put prepared work on chalk board			x
Provide a non-threatening relationship with a disturbed child	x		
Settle quarrels during play and help children to learn to share	x		
Help serve food in lunch room	x		
Assist children with boots, coats, etc.	x		
Assist the A/V director or instructional materials center supervisor with preparation, distribution and repair		x	
Assist the Librarian			x
Conduct drill sessions with flash cards	x		
Comfort a child who is physically or psychologically hurt by an aggressive peer	x		

9

SELECTION OF TEACHER AIDES

There are some functions performed by teacher aides not tied to any specific task. In ghetto schools the teacher aide from the ghetto may serve to bridge the communication gap. This is especially important when most of the teachers in the school either have had no intimate experience with ghetto living or have removed themselves from the ghetto since becoming teachers. Teacher aides in this setting are an invaluable help to teachers striving to achieve relevance in their teaching. A parallel situation exists in schools where a large proportion of the pupils have limited facility with English; where the language spoken in the home is Spanish, an Indian dialect, or a language other than English.

The use of indigenous people as teacher aides not only serves to bridge the communication gap, but is a valuable asset as a resource person for those children who are in the minority in such schools: the non-ghetto children in a ghetto school, for example. Perhaps the best lesson in meaningful integration might well be the example of a teacher and an aide representing quite different heritages cooperatively pooling their efforts in the classroom. Teachers in all schools where teacher aides are employed have an opportunity to capitalize on the wide variety of background and experience which these non-professionals bring to the school setting.

The photograph on the following page was taken during the opening moments of a teacher aide workshop. It captures the diverse composition of many teacher aide groups. The picture is also a good indicator of the positive attitudes which most teacher aides maintain toward preservice and inservice training.

Who Are the Teacher Aides?

Averages are deceiving. To give the average age for any group of people, or the marital status or amount of education is of little practical value for any particular school district. It is of value to cite the range of ages as 17-70, and the narrower age range including the greatest proportion of teacher aides as 31-40. A large majority of teacher aides are women, and most of them are married.

The formal education of teacher aides runs the gamut from less than a high school education to a college degree plus graduate work at a university. A number of school districts with which the authors are acquainted have set a minimum academic requirement of a high school diploma or its equivalent. One hundred sixty-six teacher aides from 21 school districts in Southeast Missouri who participated in one of two preparation programs developed and directed by the authors serve as an illustration of the wide range of

Workshops are important to teacher aides.

academic backgrounds to be found. The majority, 138, had graduated from high school. Of these, 24 had attended college but had earned less than sixty semester hours. Two participants had more than sixty semester hours, but less than a degree; two had college degrees and one had some graduate credit. Of the remaining 28, who did not graduate from high school, 6 had passed the G.E.D. equivalency test.

Teacher aides represent nearly every socio-economic level that is a part of the American scene today. Many are from the middle class to be sure, but both upper and lower classes are well represented.

Perhaps more descriptive than educational level, age, sex, martial status, or socio-economic level would be their personal characteristics. With few exceptions teacher aides are interested in children and their education. Teacher aides are industrious and willing workers. They serve for little pay, many for no monetary remuneration. They are interested citizens who see the school as an important social institution. For some teacher aides serving voluntarily without pay, it is a positive involvement in social action.

11

SELECTION OF TEACHER AIDES

Organizational Patterns

Teacher aides follow the existing patterns of school organizations in which they serve. This generally is elementary, junior high, and high school. In addition to these usual patterns, teacher aides find themselves in special education and clerical service positions. Thus, they are a part of the total school organization with the exception of the central office and board of education.

Many school districts and several states have provisions for quasi-certification of teacher aides with delineation of levels by academic preparation or position such as: instructional aides, clerical aides, or cafeteria aides. Most states include paid teacher aides in their retirement system for non-certified (teacher or administrator certification) personnel with custodians, cooks, secretarial, and transportation personnel.

It is the expectation of many educators, including the authors, that teacher aides will in the near future hold more clearly defined status within the school organization, and have their own separate semi-professional organization. Further, the formal education requirements for the top level positions, especially instructional, in which they serve will increase. It is the hope of these writers that academic entrance requirements will not increase correspondingly. Our experience in working with teacher aides has increased our respect for them as people interested in children and schools. They have a valuable contribution to make.

How Teacher Aides are Recruited

There are many methods by which teacher aides are recruited. The size and location of the school district and certain atypical reasons for attracting a particular type of person to this service are factors influencing recruitment methods. If it is important to employ ghetto people to bridge the communication or relevance gap as well as to perform the usual task, it might be expedient to "spread the word" through organizations in contact with those who live in the ghetto. In a small, relatively isolated rural district the principals and teachers need only whisper once among themselves and the entire community will be aware of the need—and those interested will present themselves. In a city or metropolitan district of some size the conventional news media may serve best.

Whether the need is announced through organizations, made known by word-of-mouth, or advertised conventionally, a formal application in writing is necessary.

The Written Application

   The application serves as a criteria for selection and a source of personal information. Included is the usual numerical information such as: age, social security number, years of education, number of children, etc. Of equal importance should be an account of personal experiences of value in a school environment, and personal reasons for offering to serve as a teacher aide. Two sample application forms used by schools known to the authors are included here. They are different in length and type of information requested. One seeks specific skills and the other does not. They were taken from a town, and a medium sized city school district. There are as many forms and styles of applications as there are school districts employing teacher aides. Either of these examples may serve as a point-of-departure for an administrator who must develop a first application or revise an existing application.

APPLICATION

For Teacher Aides

Home Town Public Schools

Name _____
          Last   First   Middle

Address _____ Phone _____

Social Security Number _____ Age _____

High School Attended _____ Did You Graduate? _____

College Attended _____ Years Completed _____ Major _____

Do You Type?_____ Take Shorthand? _____

Run Movie Projector?_____ Use Tape Recorder _____

   Please describe experiences you have had working with children. (Church, scouts, etc.)

Work Experience:
    Employer   Dates Employed   Type of Work

1. _____

2. _____

13

SELECTION OF TEACHER AIDES

3. _____

4. _____

Character References:

Name	Address	Position
1.		
2.		
3.		

APPLICATION

Teacher Aide

Central City School District

Name _____
        Last   First   Middle

Address _____

Years at above address _____ Phone _____

Social Security Number _____ Age _____

Marital Status _____ Number of Children _____

Did you graduate from high school? _____ If not, how many years

did you complete? _____ Give the name and city or town of the

last school you attended. _____

Have you attended a college, junior college, trade school, or served in an

apprenticeship for a skilled trade? _____ If yes, list the school, the

length of time in attendance and total credits earned:

_____
        school   time in attendance

_____ . If an apprenticeship, did you complete the
      credits earned

training? _____ If completed, when, and with what firm or union

local? _____
    date completed   firm or local

14

Please list your last two periods of employment.

1. _____
   employer   years and months
   _____
                    type of work performed

2. _____
   employer   years and months
   _____
                    type of work performed

List two references:

1. _____
   name   address
   _____
   nature of acquaintance   years known

2. _____
   name   address
   _____
   nature of acquaintance   years known

Explain briefly why you want to serve as a teacher aide.
_____
_____

Evaluation of the Written Application

Evaluation of the written application must necessarily be in terms of the particular needs of the school and the experience and skill possessed by the applicants. Beyond this, the written application serves two important purposes: as a basis for personal interview; and as a source of personal data for those applicants accepted. For the proper disposition of written applications the following suggestions are offered to school administrators:

1. Acknowledge applications received by mail immediately.

2. If references are requested, be sure you contact persons so designated by applicants.

3. Strive for diversity in personal characteristics among applicants for teacher aide positions.

4. Send a courteous notice to those applicants not employed.

SELECTION OF TEACHER AIDES

Those responsible for evaluation of applicants should give special attention to number 4, preceding. Remember, those applicants not chosen for employment are interested in the school; and those interested applicants are still contributing citizens who will remain in the community over the years.

Hints for Applicants

Those who may be considering serving as teacher aides should include as much favorable information on the application as appropriate. Keep in mind that children are the primary citizens in the schools, and those who teach the children are next in order of importance. The aspiring teacher aide applicant must think in terms "how can I help." An applicant who presents herself as flexible and eager to learn will have an edge.

Few who enter service as teacher aides have extensive training especially designed to prepare persons for the tasks performed by aides. Thus, the personal characteristics of applicants loom important. The characteristics usually sought by schools are: dedicated, compassionate, likes children, flexible, responsive to teachers, able to get along, and personable. A sincere desire to improve one's self, and to learn to perform the tasks assigned will put the new teacher aide in a favorable position for true service.

The Interview

The value of a personal interview in the selection of persons applying for any position in schools is well known. Such important factors as voice, facial expressions, personal grooming, attitude toward children, sense of humor, poise, and physical size can best be observed in person. These factors are of prime importance for persons who will work in schools and have contact with children.

In addition to an interview with the person responsible for official employment offers, it is important to take the prospective teacher aide on a tour of the facilities; even though it is the applicant's 'home town' and she has children in school. If possible, introduce the applicant to other teacher aides and to teachers with whom she may be working. An expression of support or rejection by those to whom the applicant is thus introduced, especially teachers, may be of value in the decision to offer a position. It is the opinion of these authors that teachers should have a strong voice in the selection of aides who will work closely with them.

16

*A Two-Fold Responsibility: Teacher Aide to School,
and School to Teacher Aide*

Probably no other position in education is filled by such a broad cross-section of people from the general population. Nor filled by people of whom so few entrance requirements in terms of specific skills or academic preparation are expected. Thus, the importance of becoming educated for the tasks to be performed after acceptance for the position, is the more magnified. It is the first responsibility of the new teacher aide to seek avenues of self-improvement and mastery of specific skills. There are education and training opportunities for teacher aides in evening schools, adult education classes, and college-sponsored workshops. The new teacher aide has the responsibility to seek out these opportunities and pursue them.

Conversely, the school has a responsibility for facilitating the pursuance of preparation programs by teacher aides, and encouraging teacher aides to avail themselves of any opportunities provided. It is less than wise to expect non-professional aides to serve efficiently with no formal preparation for the specific tasks they are asked to perform. Since, in fact, this is usually the case the school district acts in the best interests of the children by doing the next best thing: provide the impetus for the development of programs designed to prepare teacher aides for service in their schools. This responsibility must be considered at all stages in the process of selection of teacher aides.

CHAPTER III

PREPARATION PROGRAMS

Present practice by school districts in which teacher aides serve is to train the aides after they begin serving. This in-service training is usually effected in one of three ways: An informal on-the-job trial period during which teachers, administrators and experienced aides "show them the ropes"; 2) a two or three day preschool orientation developed and directed by an administrator in the building or several administrators from the entire school district. This may be concurrent with the preschool orientation for new teachers; or 3) a one or two week workshop developed and directed by personnel outside the school district, usually from a nearby institution of higher education.

At this writing, the authors know of no school district where the criteria for selection as a teacher aide includes a specified period of formal training. Such requirements would be a handicap in schools where some teacher aides are recruited primarily for non-task-oriented functions. (See Chapter II.)

There is, however, a discernible trend toward programs of preparation developed to meet the minimal needs of teacher aides. This trend is a result of Federal funds made available to local school districts through Title I, and funds available to institutions of higher education via Part B, Subpart 2, of the Education Professions Development Act. The latter limits participation to new teacher aides, and requires that at least two weeks of the preparation (training) program be completed prior to service in the school. This does not prescribe local district selection criteria inclusive of pre-service preparation, but it may be a gentle nudge in that direction.

PREPARATION PROGRAM

The absence of any prescribed program of preparation, the success of in-service training programs that have been developed, and the impetus of federal funding for the hiring of teacher aides have resulted in the evolvement of distinct patterns of in-service training for teacher aides. The less-frequent pre-service preparation programs have tended to develop in these same modes. A brief description of these patterns of preparation programs are presented here. The reader is expected to be cognizant of the applicability of each type of program for both pre-service preparation and in-service training. It is further expected that those charged with the responsibility of initiating such programs have insight into the practical value of including the teachers with teacher aides in those training sessions relative to the development of cooperative understanding of school problems.

The Preparation Program — On Campus

The advantages of conducting a pre-service preparation program, an in-service institute, or even a short workshop on campus are four-fold: First, the facilities of an institution of higher education, whether a two-year institution, four-year institution or a university are usually more extensive than those of a local school district. Second, when drawing upon the expertise of a professional faculty, it is expedient in terms of choice of professors, and the amount of time and energy they can devote to the program to meet them on their home ground. Third, the teacher aide will feel freed of the environmental pressures of the home and school, and thus concentrate more intently on the lessons presented. Fourth, the psychological impact of the campus milieu will exert a positive motivational force on the teacher aides in the program.

Most pre-service programs of preparation for teacher aides are held on the campus of an institution of higher education. On-campus programs of in-service education commonly developed for teacher aides during the summer are usually of one to three weeks duration. Colleges are better able to house and feed a large group when a large proportion of their full-time students are away. The normal academic load of professors is often somewhat less demanding during the summer session. These factors increase the opportunity for many professors to make a contribution to the in-service education program for teacher aides. One further advantage may accrue when teachers and teacher aides live together and work together for one or more weeks on a college campus: it is easy to determine the degree of compatibility which a teaching team may enjoy throughout the school year.

The Preparation Program — In the Local School Setting,
Conducted by Higher Education Personnel

Certain advantages accrue to the teacher aides and their school district when the college brings the program to the school. Primarily, the professors have an opportunity to experience the environment in which the teacher aides serve. This experience tends to alter the content and presentation of the lesson taught; resulting in greater relevance of knowledge and skills learned by teacher aides. Of secondary importance is the inclusiveness of programs brought to the local school district. Every teacher aide can be required to participate, and teachers can also be asked to attend appropriate sessions.

The Preparation Program — In the Local School Setting, Conducted
by Their School Personnel using Higher Education Consultants

The single most advantageous aspect of this type of in-service training program is that it is "home grown" and "tailor made" by and for the local school district. Local school districts with well qualified personnel in many positions are capable of conducting a meaningful preparation program for teacher aides, and following through with an in-service program during the first year of service. The limited use of consultants from outside the district will "shore up" apparent weaknesses in local talent. A positive observation by the authors has been the greater degree of meaningful involvement and cooperative spirit displayed by the faculty and building administrators when this type of program is initiated.

Similarities of Preparation Programs

The above described patterns of preparation programs for teacher aides have in common certain goals, procedures and possibilities. In all of the above the goal is optimum performance of tasks by teacher aides through a program of pre-service and/or in-service training. In all three preparation programs there should be provision for cooperative learning experiences in which teachers are included with the teacher aides. Further, it is logical to involve teachers in decisions regarding the "curriculum" of the preparation program. They should know best which competencies aides need, and should help in establishing priorities. Those closest to the action understand best the demands made upon the aides, and the order of importance for each task.

There are several possibilities for providing either pre-service or in-service preparation for teacher aides at a minimum expense to the school district or the teacher aide. Many people with valuable experience and ex-

21

pertise will serve voluntarily as consultants, lecturers, demonstration technicians or instructors. Most State Departments of Education, institutions of higher education, large business firms and large public agencies have professional personnel available for such endeavors. There are also federal education programs that support the training of teacher aides. Many training programs have been funded under provisions of Title I, of E.S.E.A. Some are currently being conducted through State Education Department plans supported financially through Part II-B, of the E.P.D.A. This is a federal program of assistance for preparation programs planned jointly by state departments of education and institutions of higher education. In some school districts training programs for teacher aides have received financial support from local organizations interested in the school. Of course, it is not regarded as imprudent for individual school districts to absorb the cost of training their aides. In schools where teacher aides receive remuneration for their services it does not seem unreasonable to expect them to make some contribution toward their own training program. Presently salaries, when paid, are such that the aide's contribution is her time.

Twenty Valuable Lessons — With Outlines of Lesson Plans

Experience has proven the worth of each lesson described herein. Most are appropriate for pre-service preparation programs, some are better included in programs of in-service training, and other lessons may be included in locally managed on-going training programs with excellent results. An indication of appropriate program organization for optimum results is included with each lesson discussed and outlined.

Lesson 1

The Role of the State in Education

The Rationale: A greater degree of cooperative effort by administrators, classroom teachers, special teachers and teacher aides is possible when all members of the education team understand the authority, organizational purposes, and specific local goals of education in today's society.

The Outline:

I. The Philosophical and Legal Foundation

    A. Some definitive purposes of public education in contemporary America.
       1. the realization of self-potential

    2. understanding the nation, state and local environment

    3. human purpose and progress in the world

B. The constitutional authorization for public education

    1. delegated responsibilities to the states

    2. the local school district board of education

    3. the superintendent

    4. supervisory personnel

    5. building principals

    6. teachers

    7. auxiliary personnel — teacher aides

C. The development of teacher aide programs

    1. state provisions and requirements

    2. classifications of teacher aides

      a. instructional

      b. non-instructional

    3. some examples of tasks by classification

    4. responsibility for teacher aide programs

      a. administrative

      b. the classroom teacher

      c. the teacher aide

    5. group discussion of the need for organizing, planning and implementing the teacher aide program

    6. group discussion of problems encountered in teacher aide service

      a. causes

      b. alternatives for resolution of problems

This lesson is especially appropriate for pre-service preparation programs. Two fifty-minute sessions are sufficient to teach this lesson. A brief evaluation can be included in this time period. This evaluation should include more than just the lesson. It should be a point of assessment regarding the lessons to follow, and include interrelationships of the teaching community including the teacher and teacher aide. At this point some changes of format, method, or instructional personnel may be made which would be advantageous to the participants throughout the remainder of the workshop or institute.

Lesson 2

Community Resources

The Rationale: The local school exists in the larger community environment. Just as the function of the school extends throughout the school community, so do the resources for education and experience within the community extend to the school. All members of the education team, including teacher aides, should be aware of these resources. Community resources to which the local school may turn are defined as: local sources to help in securing improved education and physical well-being for the child in school.

The Outline:

I. Physical well-being

A. Health agency resources
   1. local health department
   2. crippled children agency
   3. local or regional centers for retarded or emotionally disturbed children
   4. county health department
      a. immunization programs
      b. hearing testing
      c. vision testing
      d. tuberculosis prevention
      e. water supply
      f. safety programs

B. Social agency resources
   1. Private
      a. family service agencies=(sectarian and non-sectarian)
      b. adoption service
   2. Governmental
      a. welfare department
      b. employment security commission

II. Improvement of education

A. Parents
   1. breaking communication barriers
   2. participation in school activities
   3. interest in and acceptance of homework

B. Volunteers
   1. fund raising and booster clubs
   2. field trips and other school functions
   3. little league and other non-school sport organizations
   4. culture----local artist, musicians, etc.

C. Local business, government and institutions, and natural resources
   1. field trip invitation and planning

D. Indirect resources (available through school administrative channels)
   1. school board
   2. community power structure

This lesson would be of most value to the teacher aide after service to the school has begun. The information could best be taught by a professional social worker. The time requirements of the lesson would not exceed two fifty-minute periods including the brief evaluation.

Lesson 3

School Public Relations

The Rationale: By virtue of the term 'public', the citizens of all public school districts think possessively about 'their' schools. People expect to know about their possessions whether individual and private, or collective and public. Complex institutions (schools) owned collectively by the public send out messages concerning their function in many ways. Some of these 'messages' are planned; and some are incidental. Often, the important 'messages' received by the general public are transmitted via members of the institution. Teacher aides are members of such an institution when serving in the school. Thus, they have the responsibility of understanding their role in the transmittal of messages.

The Outline:

I. Some questions that need answers.

   A. What is school public relations?

   B. Are teacher aides involved in school public relations?
      1. If so, how?

   C. A definition: school public relations is the combined effort of students, teachers, auxiliary personnel (teacher aides), and administrators, to tell the school story "like it is" in their community.

II. Typical publications circulated within and outside of the school and their PR function.

   A. Notices

   B. Bulletins

25

C. Special reports

D. Annual reports

E. School papers

F. Yearbooks

III. Verbal means of transmitting information about the school

   A. The transmitters:
     1. children
     2. staff members — including teacher aides
     3. teachers
     4. administrators

   B. Circumstances of verbal communication
     1. oral reports to parents
     2. conversation with friends
     3. visits to other institutions, agencies or organizations
     4. gossip ------

IV. Some role playing exercises for teacher aides

   A. The teacher aide reacts to this statement: (local store owner)— "Some of my customers have told me of how the children like you much better than the teacher. They think you should be the teacher, and Miss Jones should be the aide."
     1. Other teacher aides in the class rate the appropriateness of the aide's reaction to the statement on a four point scale: 1, 2, 3, and 4. (1 = highest, 4 = lowest)
     2. each rating requires a one or two sentence justification

   B. The teacher aide reacts to this statement from an acquaintance at a Saturday evening social event attended by fifteen other people: (the acquaintance)— "Say, I hear there is a real feud in the school where you work. I understand the assistant principal has it in for Mr. Smith (a teacher) and the other teachers have come to his (Mr. Smith's) defense."
     1. Other teacher aides in the class rate the appropriateness of the aide's reaction to the statement on a four point scale: 1, 2, 3, and 4. (1 = highest, 4 = lowest)
     2. each rating requires a one or two sentence justification

   C. The teacher aide reacts to this declaration from a child: (the child)— "Gosh, Mrs. Robert, you teach me lots better than cranky

26

ole Miss Smith. She doesn't like me, and I want you to help me with my reading instead of her."

1. Other teacher aides in the class rate the appropriateness of the aide's reaction to the statement on a four point scale: 1, 2, 3, and 4. (1 = highest, 4 = lowest)
2. each rating requires a one or two sentence justification.

This lesson is equally appropriate for pre-service preparation programs for teacher aides, or in-service training programs. The understanding of concepts and specific information or experiences are to be desired at the beginning of service, but may be more meaningful and easier to learn after the teacher aid has been in service a few weeks. Parts I, II, and III, of this lesson could be learned in one fifty-minute session. Part IV, could be completed in thirty minutes. A brief evaluation in which a summary of A, 1 and 2; B, 1 and 2; and C, 1 and 2, are included could be accomplished in an additional thirty minutes.

Lesson 4

The United States Office of Education

The Rationale: It is important that teacher aides be knowledgeable of the educational framework in which they are working. In recent years the influence of the federal government in education at all levels has increased significantly. It is logical to expect teacher aides to be more dedicated in their service when they have some comprehension of the total educational enterprise.

The Outline:

I. The history of the creation and authority of the U.S. Office of Education.

II. The structural organization of the U.S. Office of Education within the framework of the Department of Health, Education, and Welfare.

III. The purposes and organization of the U.S. Office of Education.

A. Staff officers and service elements
1. office of equal educational opportunity
2. office of programs for the disadvantaged
3. office of construction service
4. national center for educational statistics
5. associate commissioner for field service

B. Program bureaus
  1. elementary and secondary education
  2. adult and vocational education
  3. higher education
  4. research
  5. education for the handicapped

IV. The role of the federal government in public education and the function of the U.S. Office of Education in this role.

V. The relationship of the U.S. Office of Education to the states.

This lesson would be appropriate to include in a pre-service preparation program for teacher aides. The lesson would of necessity be primarily lecture. It is suggested that the presentation be made by staff personnel from the State Education Department. Most state departments have well qualified people who give this type of service to local school districts. The wise use of visual aids with this lesson would serve to increase interest in the presentation. Two fifty-minute sessions are usually needed to make the presentation, provide the teacher aides an opportunity for questions and interaction, and to complete a meaningful written evaluation.

Lesson 5

The Psychological Orientation of the Teacher's Aide

The Rationale: Much of the learning process is organized on psychological principles. Certified personnel in public schools are required to complete one or more courses of study in psychology or in professional education courses with a psychological orientation. Teacher aides cannot long serve in an environment in which the basis for methodology is psychological in nature without developing a healthy curiosity about the "reasons why teachers and administrators proceed with their tasks of education as they do."

This lesson, or group of lessons, has proven an invaluable asset to teacher aids in their daily contact with the observation of children in school. Although some educators would frown upon anything less than an in-depth study of psychology, it must be remembered that most people serving as teacher aides have at least a cursory background in psychology; though usually not as a result of formal education. Popular magazines, newspapers and television programs are a constant source of information in the field of psychology. These articles and television shows run the gamut from child rearing or causes and treatment of delinquent youth to lengthy two-part specials on the life and work of Sigmund Freud.

These lessons dealing with psychology are an attempt to synthesize the psychological facts already understood by teacher aides, add to this knowledge, and apply the whole to the teaching-learning process.

The Outline:

I. Intelligence

  A. What we measure (specific behaviors)
    1. intelligence as a factor in the traditional school program
    2. intelligence as a factor in recent innovative programs in the school

  B. Improvement of the I.Q.
    1. learning or learned behaviors
      a. vocabulary
      b. information
      c. skills
    2. physical well-being
    3. social knowledge

  C. Creativity
    1. as a function of intelligence
    2. common at all levels
    3. maintaining creativity

II. Learning

  A. Basic assumptions
    1. behavior is observed, learning is inferred
      a. intelligence
      b. motivation
      c. physical condition
      d. past experience

  B. Elements of all learning
    1. Association
      a. the presence of two or more stimuli
      b. the value of reinforcement
    2. Generalization
      a. recognition of similarities in situations
      b. the attempt to "try out" new learning

      3. Discrimination
         a. recognition of differences between situations
         b. extinction of incorrect responses

III. Motivation

  A. The motivational process
     1. needs and behavior
     2. sex needs
     3. desire for activity

  B. Reinforcement in learning
     1. purpose or intent to learn
     2. knowledge of progress and results
     3. self-concept

  C. Goals and incentives
     1. rewards
     2. punishment
     3. competition
     4. feelings of achievement and success
     5. social approval
     6. vocational goals

IV. Frustration

  A. A definition of frustration

  B. Sources of frustration
     1. practical situations — some examples
     2. social order
     3. the individual himself

  C. Withdrawal reactions to frustration
     1. fantasy
     2. nomadism
     3. repression

  D. Aggressive reaction to frustration
     1. displaced aggression
        a. scapegoating
        b. free-floating anger
        c. suicide
     2. identification
     3. projection

      E. Frustration in the classroom

V. Testing

    A. Purposes of testing
        1. obtain indications of maturity level
        2. obtain indications of what the child has learned
        3. for placement

    B. Some examples of intelligence test items from the Wechsler intelligence scale for children

    C. The relationship of intelligence and achievement

VI. Perception

    A. The definition

    B. Elements of perception
        1. Sensation
           a. sensory acuity
           b. completeness of stimulus

        2. Thought
           a. intelligence
           b. experience
           c. attitude
           d. physical state

    C. Distortion of perception
        1. influence of past experience
        2. expectancy
        3. body needs

    D. Developing accurate perception
        1. accurate observation
        2. tentative judgment

This lesson would be appropriate for either the pre-service or in-service preparation of teacher aides. It should be included as part of the aides' general instruction, and would be equally effective in all three patterns of preparation discussed in the first section of this chapter. This lesson has been included in several institutes and workshops, both pre-service and in-service. Several instructors have combined to develop this psychology lesson into a presentation relevant for teacher aides. The possibilities for variety of teaching methods are easily recognized by a psychology teacher with a modicum of ability and experience. Pre-test, post-test experiences; small group problem-identification sessions; role-playing, audio-visual aids, and lecture-discussion techniques have all been used with success.

This psychology lesson is best taught in eight fifty-sixty minute sessions presented on four different days. If the four days are at weekly or bi-monthly intervals, some review is necessary at the beginning of the 2nd, 3rd, and 4th days of the lesson. A glossary of terms and list of example situations should be provided the teacher aides at the beginning of the lesson. Also, a synopsis of each lesson given at the close of each lesson will serve as reinforcement for those teacher aides who will use it as a review. There is, of course, no text or formal reading assignment. This condition, and the fact that most teacher aides in attendance are not practiced at note-taking are reasons for using as many hand-out materials as can be developed and used.

Lesson 6

Playground Supervision

The Rationale: One of the non-instructional chores most readily relinquished by classroom teachers is that of playground supervision. Indeed, this taxing duty, according to most classroom teachers, is justification enough for implementing a program of teacher aide service. There are still some educators, lay leaders, and administrators who do not believe a non-certified person should ever be left in charge of a group of school children. To this the majority point to the bus transportation of pupils to and from school, and to such non-school activities as scouting, 4-H Clubs, little league, and others supervised by adults without a "magic" certificate;—and they are accepted by parents. Most teachers and administrators believe that with an understanding of acceptable guidelines and reasonable care teacher aides may serve well as playground supervisors.

The Outline:

I. The Responsibilities of the Playground Supervisor

A. Be aware of what is going on.

B. Be alert to prevent children from engaging in careless practices—throwing the bat in a softball game.

C. Remind children when necessary that good manners and sportsmanlike conduct must prevail.

D. Help children to care for playground equipment.

32

E. Be available to answer questions and offer assistance if needed.

F. Enforce regulations. These should be few, simple, and reasonable.

G. Be firm and consistent, but kind, in dealing with offenders of playground regulations.

II. Some Typical Playground Problems

    A. Aggressive children infringe on the rights of others — timid children are pushed aside.

    B. Roughness may occur
       1. teasing
       2. tripping
       3. pushing
       4. fighting

    C. Older children may lead younger ones into danger or mischief

    D. Undesirable language may be used

    E. Equipment and space may be misused

    F. Quarreling over spaces, equipment, members of teams

III. Examples of Suitable Play Activities

    A. Playing on playground apparatus

    B. Individual and small group activities
       1. rope jumping
       2. hop scotch
       3. ball bouncing
       4. playing "catch"
       5. tether ball
       6. four-square

    C. Examples of running games
       1. tag
       2. races
       3. red light
       4. relays
       5. steal the bacon
       6. slap jack
       7. midnight

    D. Some low organization team games
        1. dodge ball
        2. kick ball
        3. goal soccer
        4. touchdown—running only

    E. Popular team games
        1. softball
        2. volleyball

IV. Unsuitable Play Activities

    A. Dangerous or difficult to supervise
        1. wrestling
        2. rock throwing
        3. crack the whip

    B. Example of misuse of playground apparatus—cause of injury
        1. two in one swing
        2. jumping out of swings
        3. running under swing
        4. pushing others off the slide or jungle gym

V. To Encourage Shy or Awkward Children to Play

    A. Play with them (brief periods) enthusiastically

    B. Suggest some simple activities
        1. teach them how to play
        2. show them the activities are safe

    C. Stress fun

    D. Suggest things to do alone or with one or two others

VI. Cliques on the Playground—Suggestions

    A. Allow them to play together unless
        1. they interfere with the rights of others
        2. they disrupt the progress of the game

    B. Arrange to distribute them among groups occasionally

    C. Play with them
        1. If two are troublesome, take a position between them

VII. Avoid Serious Accidents

   A. Plan activities in advance and assign areas that are adequate and safe

   B. Check equipment and apparatus daily for safety

   C. Clear play area of sticks, stones, and hazards such as holes

   D. Position the groups far enough apart for safety, but near enough for supervision

   E. Arrange for children to play with their own grade, or age group

   F. Mark lines, circles, hop scotch, shuffleboard, and other on hard top, sidewalks or hallways.

VIII. What You Should Do in Case of Accident

   A. If there is a written school policy concerning accident situations, learn it thoroughly and abide by it

   B. Unless school policy is contrary:
      1. Send a reliable child for the classroom teacher, nurse, or principal.
      2. If slightly injured—skinned knee—send the injured child to the teacher or nurse.
      3. Never send an injured or sick child alone—always send someone with him; another child, aide or adult staff member.
      4. Avoid crowding or hysteria of the other children—go back to the game as soon as possible.
      5. If the injury seems serious, stay with the injured child until help arrives. Cover him, talk to him; do not move him.

IX. Examples of Suitable Indoor Games and Spaces

   A. Places where games are played
      1. gymnasium
      2. classroom
      3. stage of auditorium
      4. all purpose room
      5. hallways

   B. Quiet games
      1. guessing games
      2. puzzles

       3. checkers
       4. riddles
       5. other table games

   C. Semi-active games
       1. relays
       2. hop scotch
       3. jacks
       4. bean bag and other tossing games

   D. Singing games and simple rhythm activities

This lesson deals with one of the specific tasks performed by teacher aides. It is appropriate for either pre-service or in-service preparation programs, and can easily be included in any of the three patterns of preparation discussed earlier in this chapter. The most successful presentations of this lesson have been made by persons with experience in playground supervision at the elementary level and formal training in physical education. This is one of the lessons taught with optimum effectiveness when teachers and teacher aides are included in the same workshop session.

There are ready sources of information inclusive of games and activities appropriate for playground, gymnasium, or classroom; during lunch periods or recess periods. These sources include: state departments of education, state college or university physical education departments, and professional associations within the National Education Association.

This lesson requires at least two fifty-minute sessions. It should not be taught by the lecture method alone. There are several excellent films on playground activities which would serve well as an introduction to this lesson. Of proven worth is a participation technique where each aide has practice in dealing with common problems of playground supervision in a simulated situation; — an enlarged role-playing technique. There are other 16mm films, and audio or visual materials available as a basis for group interaction concerning this multi-faceted task of playground supervision.

Lesson 7

Basic First Aid

The Rationale: Teacher aides often supervise children in an activity situation; on the playground, during noon recreation programs or indoor recess periods. For the aide — or teacher for that matter — who is the sole supervisory adult present, basic first aid training is an absolute must. First aid supplies should be easily accessible in 'high risk' areas, and teacher aides should be familiar with them.

The Outline:

I. The First Thing to Do in Case of Emergency - General

    A. Keep the patient lying down, his head level with the rest of his body unless there is suspected head injury, then raise his head slightly.

    B. Don't move him.

    C. Make sure that air passages are open—wipe out the back of his throat with your finger if the passage is blocked.

    D. Make sure he is breathing—if not tilt his head backward, pull jaw foreward and begin mouth-to-mouth breathing.

    E. Stop any serious external bleeding by applying pressure over the wound with your hand or any material handy.

    F. Don't give him anything by mouth if he is unconscious or semi-conscious.

    G. Cover him and keep him *comfortably* warm.

II. Demonstration—Practice

    A. Mouth-to-Mouth Breathing

    B. Control of External Bleeding

    C. Counting Pulse (necessary in shock)

    D. Moving an Injured Person

    E. Splinting Broken Bones

    F. How to Handle Diabetic Emergencies

    G. How to Handle Convulsions

    H. How to Handle Allergic Reaction (shock)

    I. How to Handle Choking

    J. Using the First Aid Kit

This lesson should be introduced with one of the several excellent films available. Since the lesson is primarily one of demonstration and practice, it will require approximately three fifty-minute sessions. The supervised practice sessions are most effective when the class is divided into small sections, 10-12 each, with an instructor in attendance with each small group. There are innumerable persons capable of instructing teacher aides in the basics of first aid; registered nurses, red cross first aid instructors, physical education teachers and physicians.

This lesson is easily managed in any of the three organizational patterns for preparation programs cited earlier in this chapter. It is of importance whether included in pre-service or in-service preparation programs for teacher aides.

Lesson 8

Clerical Assistance—Machine Copying

The Rationale: Teachers have an ever increasing instructional task in this era of the knowledge explosion, satelite communications, and space exploration. The educational needs of students require teachers to use their talent and professional preparation to plan, teach, and evaluate lessons. The time and energy of teachers diverted from the teaching-learning process to clerical tasks is an expensive misappropriation of professional service that few schools can afford. These important support tasks can be performed satisfactorily by teacher aides; and at an hourly rate far below that earned by a certified teacher.

The Outline:

   I. The Spirit Duplicating Process

      A. Parts of master unit

      B. Preparing masters

      C. Making corrections

      D. Drawing on masters

      E. Running off the copies

      F. Re-use of the master
         1. correct preparation for storage

  II. The Mimeograph Process

      A. Parts of the stencil

      B. Preparing the guide copy

    C. Placement of copy on stencil

    D. Typing the stencil

    E. Making corrections

    F. Handwork on stencils

    G. Running off the copies

    H. Storage of the stencils for re-use

III. The Thermal Spirit Master Unit

    A. Preparing the thermal master unit

    B. Operation of the Thermo-Fax — "The Secretary"
       1. running off copies

IV. The Care of Machines — Preventive Maintenance

    A. The typewriter

    B. The spirit duplicator

    C. The mimeograph

    D. The thermal spirit master units

This task-oriented lesson is appropriate for inclusion in pre-service or in-service preparation programs. It is easily managed in all three patterns of program organization discussed earlier in this chapter.

The lesson should be taught by the demonstration — laboratory method. A class of twenty-five to thirty teacher aides can be accommodated in the demonstration of the step-by-step operation of each of these machines. Class division into eight or ten teacher aides is necessary for optimum effectiveness of the laboratory sessions. The provision of two pieces of equipment for each of the laboratory groups will improve the effectiveness of this experience. The instructor can easily supervise two persons as they learn to do by doing. Each teacher aide should complete each of the copying processes individually. Those who experience awkwardness, lack of confidence, or failure should have additional supervised practice.

This lesson can be organized into five thirty-minute modules. Two modules may be used for the demonstration portion. Teacher aides will usually be encouraged to ask questions at any time during the demonstration. One time module is usually enough for each of the laboratory sections. By conducting three laboratory sections simultaneously and rotating the small sections of the class, extra practice by teacher aides who need it can be handled without lengthening the modules.

Lesson 9

Lettering: The Art of Mechanical Printing

The Rationale: The use of signs in the library, in classrooms, or in bulletin board space can be a valuable asset in directing students' attention to instructional material, educational information, or general announcements. There is an attention drawing and motivational value attached to good signs. Some lettered cards, signs, and displays are used as teaching devices by classroom teachers. Many of these are stored and re-used from year to year.

Lettering is time-consuming. Teacher aides can learn one or two lettering techniques in a relatively short time and at little cost while learning. In some buildings where teachers share the services of an aide, it may not be necessary for every teacher aide to be accomplished at lettering. The oftener lettering is practiced, the more expertise the aide develops.

The Outline:

    I. Wrico Techniques

        A. Introduction to lettering
           1. practical uses
           2. costs
           3. 8mm film on WRICO technique

        B. Proper adjustment of the pen

        C. Purpose of the T-square

        D. Purpose of the template holder

        E. Purpose of the template

        F. Demonstration

   II. Koh-i-nor Technique

        A. Introduction to the technique
           1. practical uses
           2. costs
           3. similarities to the WRICO technique
           4. 8mm film on Koh-i-nor technique

        B. The proper arrangement of cardboard

C. Purpose of the T-Square

D. Purpose of the template holder

E. Purpose of the template

F. Demonstration

III. Laboratory Experience

A. Each class member imitates the instructor step-by-step in the use of WRICO technique.

B. Each class member letters his or her own name.
1. a check on progress and assistance is necessary during this practice session
2. equipment is properly cleaned and put away
3. class members keep their masterpieces

C. 16mm film on bulletin boards
1. review of the value of lettering in bulletin board display—as seen in the film

D. Each class member imitates the instructor step-by-step in the use of the koh-i-nor technique

E. Each class letters a phrase of his or her own choice

1. check of progress, and assistance if necessary, by instructor during this practice session
2. equipment is properly cleaned and put away

These particular lettering techniques are suggested because of their practicability, ease of manipulation, low cost, and frequency of use in schools. This lesson is appropriate for both pre-service and in-service preparation programs for teacher aides. It can easily be included in any of the three patterns of programs discussed in this chapter.

The lecture-demonstration-laboratory method, plus the use of three films demands that a three hour time block be used. A short "break" can be included after the film on bulletin boards. An assistant to the instructor will facilitate the handling of equipment during the demonstration and laboratory sessions. It is suggested that each teacher aide in attendance be provided the experience of cleaning and putting away the equipment at the close of the laboratory periods.

The use of large and small groups is most important. The large group provides the opportunity to explain principles, theory and to draw generalizations. The small group work provides individual aides an opportunity to apply generalizations to specific problems or experiences which will be unique to each aide's assigned tasks.

In picture "A" below, the media instructor is leading the large group of teacher aides in a generalization concerning the mechanics of printing. Picture "B" (pg. 43) shows the individual aide applying knowledge gained, in the large group instructional period, to a personal problem which requires mechanical lettering.

"A"

"B"

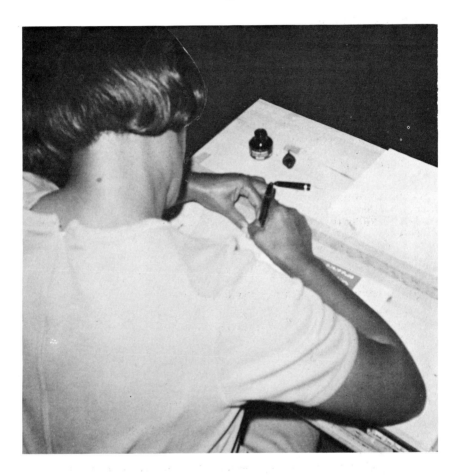

Lesson 10

Mounting: Visual Aids

The Rationale: The professional teacher is practiced in choosing the correct methods and materials for the presentation of lessons. Further, the teacher knows which materials to use and how to use them. When it is appropriate to use pictures, charts, graphs, or other visual materials that must be mounted, it is prudent to assign this task to the teacher aide.

PREPARATION PROGRAM

The Outline:

I. Rubber Cement

    A. Explanation of appropriate uses

    B. The proper use of the paper cutter
       1. safety precautions

    C. Two techniques
       1. for temporary mounting
       2. for permanent mounting

    D. Demonstration

II. Dry Mounting

    A. The appropriate use of the dry mount press

    B. Cutting to size

    C. Tacking

    D. Temperature control of dry mount press

    E. Time lapse control

    F. Demonstration

III. Laboratory

    A. Practice for each class member — rubber cement

    B. Practice for each class member — dry mount press

    C. Clean up time
       1. class members keep the materials they have mounted

This lesson is easily accomplished in two thirty-minute lecture-demonstration periods and an additional sixty-minute laboratory-practice period. For classes of more than twenty teacher aides an assistant to the instructor will facilitate the handling of equipment and supplies.

This lesson is appropriate for both pre-service and in-service preparation programs for teacher aides. It may be incorporated into nearly any organization of either of the above programs. It has proven most effective when taught by an experienced instructional materials person, or a classroom teacher with experience and expertise in the two techniques outlined.

Lesson 11

Projector Operation and Use

The Rationale: In organizing lessons, choosing materials, and developing methods of techniques for presentation the classroom teacher of the late sixties and early seventies has at her command a wealth of non-textbook information. Information projected on a screen is natural for a generation of youth brought up with television. The phenomena of 'focused' attention by an entire class is known to all present-day teachers. Lessons that can be presented as well with one of the several types of projection are less effort and more effectively taught thus, than by the lecture method. Instead of telling students about it, show it to them!

Planning the lesson and selecting appropriate materials are the prerogative of the teacher. Making room preparations for projection, setting up the projector, operation of the projector and returning the projector and materials to storage are necessary tasks that can be performed by the teacher aide. Thus, the teacher's time and energy are conserved for instruction.

The Outline:

    I. Characteristics of Projected Images

        A. Lighting—darkening

        B. Screen position

    II. Characteristics of Film

        A. The material

        B. Care of film when in use

    III. Basic Techniques of Projector Operation

        A. 16mm motion picture projector
           1. loading film
           2. focusing
           3. sound level adjustment

        B. 8mm loop (single concept) film projector

        C. Film strip projector

        D. Carrousel slide projector

        E. Overhead projector

F. Opaque projector

G. Troubleshooting projectors
    1. the plug and connection
    2. the exciter lamp
    3. the lense lamp
    4. the lense cover
    5. the sound adjustment
    6. the switches — on-off

H. Demonstration of projectors

IV. Laboratory: Equipment Operation

A. Supervised individual practice

    1. 16mm motion picture projector
    2. 8mm loop (single concept) film projector
    3. film strip projector
    4. carrousel slide projector
    5. overhead projector
    6. opaque projector

This lesson requires a minimum of three fifty-minute periods for the lecture-demonstration session and four thirty-minute laboratory sessions. It is possible to include forty to sixty class members in the lecture-demonstration period. The laboratory periods can accommodate ten to fifteen class members with good results.

This lesson is most efficiently managed in a facility large enough for both large group and small group instruction, and proximity to projector equipment, viewing apparatus (screens), and adequate electrical outlets. When the size of this class is larger than thirty-five it may be necessary to program this lesson in conjunction with another. Few schools can accommodate the equipment and physical facilities needed for a very large class for projector operation. It is appropriate for either pre-service or in-service preparation of teacher aides. Providing sufficient physical facilities and equipment are available, it could easily be included in most patterns of preparation programs for teacher aides.

Small group instruction when teaching equipment operation is most valuable. Many aides may be quite apprehensive around strange equipment. Through the workings of small groups they acquire two benefits. First, each teacher aide has more opportunity to get directly and personally involved, and secondly the aides provide mutual support for each other.

Two aides, in the picture below, are watching another aide attempt to thread a 16mm projector. The aides observing will not duplicate many of the mistakes they see their fellow aide commit, still, if they do, it will be easy to rationalize. By working in small groups errors and mistakes can be laughed off and treated as true learning experiences.

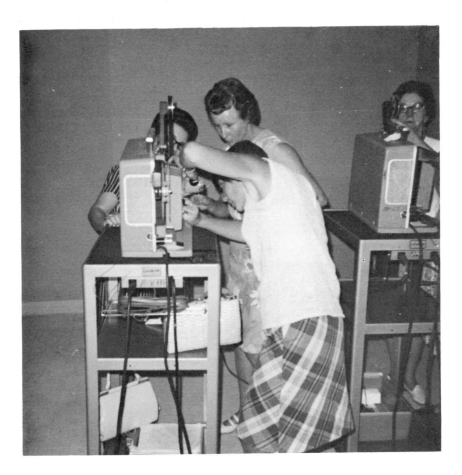

Lesson 12

Audio Recording

The Rationale: The use of audio recording via magnetic tape adds a dimension in experience, storage and retrieval, and instructional information

47

with which students can be actively involved. The use of pre-recorded tapes for instruction, story telling or factual review is common at all levels. The instruction-experience value in special classes or subject matter study is considered essential. For example: speech therapy, dramatics, public speaking classes, and foreign language classes.

The teacher aide able to prepare the classroom for tape recorder use, operate the machine, and store the tapes systematically will save valuable teacher time for instruction.

The Outline:

    I. Tape Recording

        A. Tape characteristics
           1. one-track and two-track tapes
           2. reverse of tape
           3. fragile
           4. a-splicing

        B. Microphone characteristics
           1. components
           2. position

        C. Recording with a microphone

        D. Tape rewind and playback
           1. the position dial in feet

        E. Making duplicate tapes
           1. from tapes
           2. from records

        F. Storage—do's and don't's
           1. recorders
           2. tapes
           3. record players
           4. records

   II. Laboratory: Tape Recording Practice

        A. Voice recording with microphone

        B. Make tapes from records

This lesson is practical for teacher aides in any of the three types of preparation programs; either pre-service or in-service. It can be effectively learned by most in thirty minutes lecture-demonstration and ninety minutes laboratory practice. This is based on a class of thirty teacher aides.

Most school districts have the personnel and equipment necessary to teach this lesson. It is generally unsatisfactory to leave this lesson to be taught informally during school hours by the classroom teacher.

Lesson 13

Elementary Parties

The Rationale: The less direct the relationship of an activity or function to instruction the greater the opportunity for involvement by the teacher aide. Ideally, parties and other non-academic activities are of educational value. The classroom teacher is responsible for all activities in her room, academic or non-academic. By reason of certification requirements and professional preparation there are many instructional tasks that require much of the classroom teacher and little of the teacher aide. The preparation for the supervision of parties and similar relaxed funtime activities are more easily shared by the teacher and teacher aide. Indeed, the teacher aide may have as much experience with children's parties as does the teacher.

The Outline:

    I. Sponsorship

        A. School
           1. holiday parties
           2. picnics
           3. hobo day
           4. play day

        B. Parent groups: room mothers, P.T.A., etc.
           1. end of school year
           2. awards or celebrations
           3. safety patrol parties
           4. programs honoring student achievement

        C. Individual parent planned
           1. birthdays
           2. celebrations

II. School Regulations

    A. Administrative
        1. time limitations
        2. designation of location
        3. money collection
        4. gift limitations

    B. Teachers—teacher aides
        1. cooperative planning with parents
        2. cooperative planning with students
        3. designate time allotted by administration
        4. responsibility for games
            a. how many
            b. type of games
            c. space available
            d. gifts

        5. refreshments
            a. serving
            b. kind of refreshments
            c. manners
            d. cleanup

        6. decorations
            a. students
            b. teacher aides
            c. room mothers
            d. teachers

    C. The teacher aide as assistant to the teacher and/or parents
        1. joint planning
        2. joint responsibilities
            a. total involvement
            b. preparation
            c. discipline

        3. game supervision
        4. refreshments, cleanup

III. Games: Advance Planning

    A. Types of games
        1. quiet games

        2. activity games
        3. team games

    B. Requirements of games
        1. materials needed
        2. time requirements
        3. space requirements
        4. starter, score keeper or referee

IV. Elements of a Successful Party

    A. Cooperative planning

    B. Of interest to the children

    C. Conduct it within administrative guidelines and teacher-imposed rules

This lesson is especially valuable for teacher aides who have already begun serving in a school. An excellent time to include this lesson is thirty days prior to a major party. Thus, the efforts of the teacher aide may culminate in practical application. The lesson is more relevant for aides with some experience. Further, this lesson is very effective when included in workshops or institutes in which both teachers and teacher aides are enrolled.

Ideally, any of the patterns of preparation programs—on campus, in the local school district, or in the local district with local personnel serving as teachers—are sufficient for this lesson to be successfully taught. Based on experience, optimum results have been achieved when teacher aides and teachers were included in classes conducted in the local school district by personnel from an institution of higher education. Time requirements are two fifty-minute sessions: the first devoted to a thirty-minute lecture followed by a twenty-minute question and answer period, and the second period devoted to role playing, group planning of parties, or problem solving. These techniques are especially meaningful when teacher aides and teachers switch roles, or when both assume parent, student or administrator roles.

Lesson 14

Co-curricular Activities in the Secondary School

The Rationale: Co-curricular activities are recognized by educators as a valuable adjunct to the curriculum of the modern high school or junior high school. Accurate descriptions of specific activities within the co-curricular activities program are too seldom passed on to the citizenry. In addition, this program is much more flexible than the academic curriculum. The high school principal often has authority to permit minor changes in the number and organization of activities within the program, and recommendations for major changes are usually approved by the superintendent and board of education relatively quickly. Changes within the activities program are easier. than changes within the academic program. An intramural volleyball schedule can be abandoned with less uproar than may attend dropping latin from the curriculum.

It is possible to be an alumnus of the local high school of only two or three years and experience generation gap concerning the activities program. Friends, neighbors, and other acquaintances expect all persons associated with the high school to be able to give definitive answers to their questions regarding the activities program. A brief news account of the debate team's trip to the state capitol may fall short of describing the rationale for including debating in the activities program. Teacher aides will be more reliable communicators with the public, if they understand the value of the co-curricular activities program to students. A knowledge of the functions and purposes of the activities program will give aides a grasp of the total high school program as they serve in their respective capacities.

The Outline:

I. General Functions of Co-curricular Activities

A. Personal, social and educational advantages to the student
1. opportunities are provided for the pursuit of established interests and the development of new interests.
2. education for citizenship through experiences in which fellowship, cooperation, leadership, and independent action are emphasized.
3. the development of school spirit and morale
4. opportunities for satisfying the gregarious urge of children and youth are provided
5. encouragement of moral and spiritual development
6. students' mental and physical health can be strengthened
7. provision of opportunities for the social development of students
8. widen student contacts
9. opportunities are provided for the full realization of students' creativity

B. Extension of the academic program
   1. by supplementation and enrichment of classroom experiences
   2. through the exploration of new learning experiences
      a. they may eventually be incorporated into the academic curriculum
   3. additional opportunities for individual and group guidance are manifested
   4. an activities program serves to motivate students in classroom instruction

C. Contributions to the community
   1. the activities program may be a positive influence for good school and community relations
   2. this program serves to encourage favorable community interest in, and support of the total school program

D. Some comment relative to adult leadership
   1. the degree of success of the activities program depends, to a great extent, upon the intelligent and enthusiastic leadership of advisors
   2. the adult leader (teacher aide) must remember that he is primarily an advisor
   3. the advisor (adult leader) must remember that he is accountable for the results achieved by the activity for which he has assumed leadership responsibility
   4. consultants may be used to the advantage of the student in some activities
      a. the final responsibility remains with the school designated advisor
   5. teacher aides may serve well as activity advisors and may accept a full share of the responsibility, but they should not be exploited. (Scapegoated in instances of activity failure.)

This lesson is appropriate for both pre-service and in-service preparation programs for teacher aides. It may be included in any of the three patterns of program organization described herein. The lecture-discussion method may be used effectively with this information giving-attitude forming lesson. The use of visual aids and any of the several good 16mm films relevant to activities programs will add to the understanding gained by the teacher aides being taught. Time requirements are one sixty-minute lecture-discussion period and an additional thirty minutes for one or two short films.

Lesson 15

The Art Teacher's Aide

The Rationale: Students enrolled in art classes are interested in actively exploring the available mediums of expression of their creative talent. Art is a subject that demands personal experience with the material as well as instruction regarding medium, technique and materials choices. The greater the amount of student activity and quantity of materials necessary in a particular class or subject being taught, the more extensive will be the preparation of physical facilities and materials both prior to and following each lesson period.

Teacher aides serving in art instruction classes can perform important preparation and post-class tasks. The result of this task performance is translated directly into minutes and hours. These are valuable minutes of instruction and experience for each class of students, and hours of teaching for each day the teacher works at teaching art. The teacher aide preparing for service with the art teacher should be familiar firsthand with the materials, procedures, and objectives related to art instruction.

The Outline:

    I. The Role of the Art Teacher's Aide
       A. Inventory of materials
       B. Room and equipment management
       C. Student project assistance
       D. Effective resources for teaching aids
          1. identification
          2. acquisition procedures

   II. Understanding the Objectives of Art Instruction
       A. Exploratory experience
       B. Discovery and development of talent
       C. Self expression
       D. Practicality of art

  III. Demonstration of Art Materials and Activities
       A. Paper
       B. Watercolors
       C. Clay
       D. Crayon
       E. Paint
       F. Solid materials
          1. wood
          2. metal

      3. plastic
      4. plaster

IV. Laboratory: Experience with Art Materials

V. Demonstration — Practice
   A. Removal of art materials
     1. paint from clothing
     2. paint from hard surfaces

   B. Repair of equipment
     1. easel

This lesson may be included in either a pre-service or in-service preparation program and is effective within the framework of any of the patterns of preparation discussed earlier. The time requirements for optimum familiarity and understanding by teacher aides enrolled are: fifty minutes, lecture and discussion; fifty minutes, demonstration; and six, thirty-minute laboratory periods.

The lesson has proven most valuable when taught by an enthusiastic and experienced art teacher. In addition to teacher aides serving in junior high or high school art instruction departments, many teacher aides serving in elementary classrooms have reported that it was a useful lesson for them.

Lesson 16

Elementary Physical Education

The Rationale: Physical education in the elementary school necessitates · teaching children in an area or facility apart from and larger than the classroom. The task of instructing active young pupils, oftentimes by using equipment with which they have had little experience, is best accomplished with the help of a teacher aide. One of the unique characteristics of physical education is that of having two or three different groups (within the large class) actively engaged in games or exercises at the same time. It is difficult for one teacher to supervise and instruct more than one group. With the help of an aide to supervise, the teacher can devote his attention to instruction.

To be effective in serving the physical education teacher, the teacher aide must have at least rudimentary knowledge of the physical and psychological characteristics of the elementary child and the relationship of the elementary physical education program to these characteristics. Some understanding of the appropriateness of the individual lessons to the objectives of the physical education program will prepare the aide for meaningful service. The value in terms of student progress has been demonstrated repeatedly in elementary schools where teacher aides have been assigned to the physical education instructor.

The Outline:

I. A Healthy Body is a Happy Body
   A. Physical fitness is the unique responsibility of physical education
      1. component parts of physical fitness
      2. the sedentary nature of our society
      3. enthusiasm for activity needs nurture
      4. children are less physically active outside of school today than were children thirty years ago
         a. physical education programs at the elementary level must fill the gap
      5. today's children need more than thirty minutes of physical education each day

   B. "Perfect" as an ideal in physical education
      1. nationally, it would require an extensive and disciplined effort over a period of three years to develop the physical and motor potentialities of our people
      2. the basis for program content in elementary physical education should be movement exploration
      3. at the elementary level emphasis should not be placed on perfection

II. Physical Characteristics of Elementary Age Children
   A. Grades 1-3 (ages 6-8)
      1. steady growth
      2. poor endurance due to physical limitations
         a. low red blood cell count
         b. small heart in comparison to body size
         c. high pulse rate
         d. low hemoglobin content in blood
      3. strength not developed
      4. eyes not sufficiently developed to focus on fastmoving small objects
      5. gaining control of gross movements
      6. bones are soft
         a. implications for adaptive physical education

B. Grades 4-6 (ages 9-11)
1. steady increase in height and weight
2. ossification of bones is progressing
3. improved endurance
4. improved eye control
5. much advanced coordination
   a. many skills automatic
6. greater resistance to disease than at previous level
7. increased strength
   a. still surprisingly weak
8. very active — boundless energy

III. It's More Fun With Friends
  A. Grades 1-3
   1. child is egocentric
     a. little interest in team games
   2. curiosity is a strong characteristic
   3. sex differences are insignificant
   4. adult approval is more important than peer approval

  B. Grades 4-6
   1. the beginning of gregariousness
     a. gangs
     b. teams
     c. clubs
   2. can accept some leadership responsibilities
   3. team work and cooperation are in the developmental stage

IV. A Good Sport Can "Win" When He Loses
  A. Grades 1-3
   1. child is very assertive
   2. interest is chiefly in large muscle rather than small muscle activity
   3. child has needs (and drive) for exercise and activity
   4. few, if any, leadership qualities are demonstrated

  B. Grades 4-6
   1. interest is developing in competitive and fighting activities
   2. love of excitement and adventure
   3. standards and approval of peer group are of paramount importance
   4. child is less self-assertive and individualistic

V. Practice For Progress
  A. Grades 1-3
   1. short interest span—child needs a variety of activities

        2. imitation is the strongest characteristic
        3. interest is centered on the activity of the moment, rather than future outcome

   B. Grades 4-6
        1. lengthened interest — fewer activities are engaged in
        2. increased tolerance of practicing to develop skills
        3. boys like to imitate sports heros
        4. development of interest in popular American sports

VI. Program Content
   A. Grades 1-3
        1. exploration of movement
           a. find out which movements the body is capable of performing

        2. frequent change of pace and activity
        3. occasional rest periods are needed
        4. rhythmic activities are very important
        5. the fundamentals of low organization sports skills
           a. fox and geese
           b. dodge ball
           c. kick ball
           d. soccer — kick for distance

        6. ball handling skills
           a. throwing
           b. bouncing
           c. catching

        7. relays
        8. story plays and imitations
        9. swimming
      10. stunts and tumbling
           a. imitate animals

   B. Grades 4-6
        1. basic skills and "lead-up" games
        2. sport emphasis increases (with some modification)
           a. touch football

        3. aquatic activities
        4. gymnastics
           a. stunts
           b. self-testing activities

          c. apparatus

          d. trampoline

     5. rhythms remain important

VII. Physical Fitness for School and for Life

    A. Social benefits to the child who has a strong physical education background

       1. experience with youth indicates that skill in bodily activity is an important factor in group acceptance

       2. the low-skilled individual is frequently ridiculed and shunned by his peer group

    B. Emotional problems may develop when a child fails to achieve

       1. life-long social inhibitor

This lesson, like most of the lessons included in this chapter, contains information of value for teacher aides regardless of their particular assignment. For aides serving with physical education instructors it is of prime importance. It would be advantageous for these aides to have had this lesson prior to service with the physical education teacher. However, this lesson has been included with success in both pre-service and in-service preparation programs for teacher aides. All of the patterns of the preparation programs are appropriate for the inclusion of this lesson.

The lesson requires two sixty-minute periods and is most effective when accompanied with slides (projected on a screen) of pictures depicting each item presented. A short question and answer period following the presentation is valuable for teacher aides who desire clarification or amplification of some of the concepts included in the lesson. This lesson could easily be taught by most physical education teachers with experience at both the elementary and secondary levels.

Lesson 17

Physical Education in the Secondary School

The Rationale: Physical education classes and activities usually include more students than do subject matter classes. They also include activities and equipment beyond that found in an English or history class. The service of teacher aides in secondary physical education classes is a valuable asset to the instruction of students. There are many time-consuming chores attendant with physical education that may be handled by the teacher aide permitting the teacher to concentrate on instruction. The individual differences in student ability are more readily apparent in physical activity than in academic performance, and thus more urgently beg attention. The physical education teacher aide cognizant of the objectives of physical education, the physical characteristics of students at different age levels, and the methods appropriate to instructing students in physical education will serve to enlarge the possibilities for individualized instruction so urgently needed by many students.

The Outline:

I. The Physical Education Program Is
  A. An instructional program
    1. required by the state (usually)
    2. encouraged by the national government
    3. a part of the academic curriculum
    4. a requirement for high school graduation

  B. An adapted or special program
    1. physically handicapped
    2. mentally handicapped
    3. inclusion of health and safety courses

  C. Intramural program
    1. as an extension of the physical education class
    2. limited competitive sports program

  D. Interscholastic program
    1. a valuable outlet for the physically adept
    2. valuable spectator experiences for those unable to participate

II. What Can Physical Education Do for the Secondary

  A. Help attain basic educational objectives

  B. Specific objectives of physical education
    1. physical fitness (the primary objective)
    2. physical skill development
    3. satisfactory social development
    4. emotional expression and control
    5. mental health and efficiency
    6. appreciation of physical activity and well-being

III. Physical, Psychological and Social Characteristics to be Considered When Planning Activities for the Secondary Physical Education Program

  A. Junior High (7-9 grades)
    1. girls reach puberty one to two years in advance of boys
    2. girls are one to three years ahead of boys in anatomical development
    3. bones are in rapid growth
    4. there is a great difference in height and weight of students at this age
    5. strength development follows rapid growth
    6. awkwardness is frequently pronounced because of sudden growth periods
    7. maximum endurance is not yet attained
    8. circulatory system is increasing in efficiency
    9. it is the age of loyalty
      a. especially among peers
    10. increasing attention span
    11. increasing power of abstract reasoning
    12. desire for excitement and adventure
    13. fighting tendency strong in boys
    14. desire for competitive activities by both sexes
    15. lack of confidence in oneself
    16. tendency to become moody and unstable
    17. strong interest in personal appearance exhibited by girls
    18. hero worship and susceptibility to adult leadership

  B. Senior High School (grades 10-12)
    1. girls have passed through period of rapid growth
    2. some boys are still in rapid growth period
    3. strength of girls has reached peak by age 16, and declines or remains stationary after this age
    4. strength of boys increases greatly
      a. arm and shoulder strength deficient
    5. heart capable of strenuous exercise and endurance
      a. must be developed with proper conditioning
    6. motor ability and reaction time improves and coordination develops
    7. trend toward specialization of activities
    8. still an age of loyalty and cooperation
      a. personal interests and advantages gain in importance

     9. strong interest in grooming and personal appearance
   10. boys very competitive
   11. strong interest in opposite sex
   12. increased ability to participate in group planning and problem solving

IV. Physical Education Activities for the Secondary School Student

   A. Junior high school (grades 7-9)
     1. team games should predominate
     2. individual sports
       a. adequate facilities
       b. qualified instructor
       c. track and field
       d. bowling
       e. paddle tennis
       f. archery
     3. gymnastics
       a. progression from stunts learned at the elementary level
     4. rhythms — especially for girls
     5. aquatics

   B. Senior High School
     1. allow some choice in activities
     2. increased emphasis on individual or dual sports
       a. golf
       b. badminton
       c. tennis
       d. handball
       e. bowling
       f. archery
       g. track and field events
     3. co-educational activities are good
     4. increased skill emphasized with advanced student

V. The Teacher Aide's Supporting Role

   A. Equipment storage

   B. Equipment maintenance

   C. Check-out
     1. lockers
     2. baskets

D. Shower room care

E. Set-ups for special activities

F. Inventory control

This lesson can be included in either pre-service or in-service preparation programs for teacher aides. It is of value for aides whether or not they assist the physical education instructor. For those aides serving with the physical education instructor it is an advantage to have this lesson prior to service. Specific tasks which teacher aides might perform were not discussed in this lesson. It is felt that an understanding of the purposes of the program and the characteristics of the students will lend importance to the supporting role of the teacher aide in physical education instruction.

This lesson is most effectively taught by combining a series of slides projected on a screen with the lecture, and following this with a discussion session in which individuals can ask specific questions. The lecture-slide projection session requires at least sixty minutes. An additional thirty minutes is usually ample, depending on class size, for the discussion session. This lesson is most effective when taught by an experienced physical education instructor. A person who has also been assisted by a para-professional is optimum.

Lessons 18 and 19

Teacher Aide Services for Classroom Management and Communicative Skills

The Rationale: These two lessons were found to overlap extensively in several institutes, workshops and training programs with which the authors have had experience. Recent experimentation with presenting the lessons in a team-teaching mode and purposely allowing some duplication in the use of examples has proven the most efficient and effective approach. The evidence supporting this conclusion regarding the teaching of these two lessons in concert came from tests administered to the aides enrolled, solicited evaluations from teachers and administrators, and comments from the instructors who have taught these lessons separately and together.

PREPARATION PROGRAM

These lessons contain a synthesis of the purposes for which teacher aide programs are initiated, the tasks performed in the classroom, and communication of language and instructional information among teachers, students, teacher aides, parents and administrators. It is one of the basic lessons of general information and concept assimilation that should be included in programs of preparation for teacher aides.

The Outline — Part One:

I. The Purposes of Teacher Aide Services

    A. More effective teaching-learning
        1. individualized instruction
        2. provide more depth to teaching
        3. free the teacher of non-instructional tasks
           a. the teacher can concentrate on instruction

II. Some Important Individual Differences

    A. Among children
        1. ability
        2. environment
        3. experiential background
        4. parental attitudes
        5. physical
        6. emotional

    B. Among teachers
        1. educational preparation
        2. experiences with children
        3. physical stamina
        4. emotional stability
        5. social status background

III. Implications of Our Changing Society

    A. The symbol-saturated world—teeming with visual and verbal language symbols
        1. new teaching techniques
           a. I.T.A.
           b. teaching machines
           c. programed instruction
           d. computers
        2. widened use of and exposure to foreign languages

    3. television - saturation of visual and audio symbols
    4. space exploration
       a. e.g.: the new terms and symbols associated with landing two men on the moon

B. The phantom curriculum
    1. childrens books, comics, toys, games, travels, and television
    2. a wealth of recorded information from ancient history to the space age
    3. the social pressure on educators (teachers) to make their instruction relevant

C. Human relations and language skills
    1. as knowledge expands and the verbal and symbolic recording of it increases, language skills become more important
    2. children travel more often, greater distances, experience an expanded environment
    3. new words are added to the vocabulary-language usage is often faulty
    4. more studies each year in the field of linguistics

D. Linking the past to the present-relevance
    1. the ability to read, comprehend, and interpret
    2. scholars study language
       a. origin
       b. meanings
       c. effect on human behavior

IV. The Philosophy of Education Must Include Communicative Skills

A. The early years
    1. receptive language skills
       a. listening ability
       b. reading ability
    2. two-way communication skills
       a. listening
       b. speaking
       c. reading
       d. writing
    3. the language arts concept — a fusion of the language-communication skills

B. The later years
  1. strive for perfection in language arts
  2. use of talent in communication for benefit of mankind

The Outline — Part Two:

I. Supervision of Students

  A. Locations — times
    1. lunchroom
    2. hall duty
    3. bus duty
    4. recess
    5. noon hour

  B. Supervise what, how
    1. observe behavior
    2. listen to topics discussed
    3. interests of students noted
    4. application of rules of behavior
    5. activities engaged in

II. Clerical and Classroom Tasks

  A. Office machines
    1. make copies with ditto process
      a. tests
      b. skill sheets
      c. instruction sheets
    2. thermo-fax instructional materials
      a. pictures
      b. charts
      c. graphs

  B. Audio-visual materials and equipment
    1. projection of films for language experiences
    2. show film strips related to language activities
    3. use controlled reader for stories and comprehension development

  C. Recording
    1. use of records for language activities
      a. telephone procedures
      b. plays
      c. rules of communication

      d. manners

      e. reports

    2. use of tape recorder for language activities

      a. role playing

      b. record stories

      c. plays

      d. oral interpretations

D. Files and records

    1. insert material into student permanent record folder

    2. keep filed information current, accurate, and in order

    3. check and record student scores

    4. keep all student records information *confidential*

E. Collecting money

    1. some typical collections

      a. lunchroom money

      b. insurance

      c. special fund raising projects

      d. picture money

      e. money for weekly language magazines

    2. keeping accurate records

    3. shared responsibility for money collection

F. Prepared stencils

    1. duplication of skill sheets

    2. interest inventories

    3. teacher developed instructional materials

G. Develop charts and/or graphs

    1. to denote individual progress

    2. for use with overhead projector

III. Assistance in the Classroom

A. Bulletin boards

    1. structure new displays for new topics of study

    2. keep room attractive

    3. as an interest arousing or motivation source

    4. a language unit display

    5. holiday information and decoration

B. Set up equipment
   1. audio-visual machines
   2. controlled-readers
   3. single concept, cartridge loading, loop, 8mm films
   4. language kits—e.g.: S.R.A. reading lab
   5. tables and chairs—arranged for small group instruction

C. Make-up work
   1. students who have been absent
   2. oral instruction for slow readers

D. Pre-assignment
   1. individualized instruction
   2. pre-assigned lessons — future absence

E. Drill experience—small groups
   1. small group work
      a. flash cards
      b. oral spelling
   2. phonics
   3. listening skills
   4. taped discussion analysis

F. Checking papers
   1. score, note difficulties, indicate to the teacher
   2. sometimes interpret to the students
      a. usually done by the teacher

G. Assist with laboratory — reading
   1. materials handling
      a. books
      b. pencils
      c. color charts
      d. S.R.A. (or other) kits
   2. language listening stations
      a. earphones
      b. plugs
      c. switches

H. Library
   1. check out materials—language arts
   2. develop book report displays

    3. assist in choosing books
       a. interest
       b. reading level
    4. filing systems for multi-media library

I. Assist with field trips
    1. supervise children
    2. locate materials needed
    3. pre-trip planning supplies
    4. make notations for post-trip review
    5. file of information gained by children

This lesson requires two or three instructors working as a team when presented as outlined here. In addition to the lecture presentations the use of available visual aids is recommended: two or three instructors alternate making topic presentations and handling the visual aids. At the close of each part of the lesson each instructor may lead half or one-third of the class of teacher aides in discussion of the lesson. Questions are noted in these discussion sessions. They are presented during a final meeting of the entire class, and answered by each or all of the instructors.

Five thirty-minute modules are convenient in terms of time requirements. Because of the pre-planning necessary, the instructional team should come from the same institution. This lesson is appropriate for pre-service and in-service preparation of teacher aides, and usually taught by instructors from institutions of higher education.

Lesson 20

Special Classes — A Challenge for Teacher Aides

The Rationale: The wheel with the most friction gets the grease. The teachers who teach in classrooms or schools with special problems related to class size or limitations—physical, mental or social—of the individuals who comprise the class or school need help. Often the special problems are compound; two or three 'extra' educable retarded children in the class organized to help these special children. The services of trained teacher aides in special classes or schools are especially needed by those dedicated souls teaching in them. The importance of the teacher aide in these circumstances is reflected by special financial allowances in some states. Further recognition of importance is the provision of federal funds to hire teacher aides in certain of these special classes or schools.

This lesson is a must for teacher aides serving in classes with special enrollees. It is of value to all aides, regardless of assignment, who serve in school systems where special classes are provided for children with a particular common problem related to academic progress.

The Outline:

   I. The Teacher Aide and the Mentally Retarded

      A. Causes of mental retardation
        1. prenatal
        2. injury in infancy
        3. diet
        4. disease

      B. Some frequently observed characteristics of children assigned to classes (Special Education) for metally retarded
        1. attention span
        2. memory
        3. reasoning ability
        4. flexibility
        5. social development
        6. cultural background

      C. The influence of adult behavior and attitudes upon the attitudes and performance of children
        1. the 'normal' child
        2. the mentally retarded child

   II. The Teacher Aide and Disadvantaged Youth

      A. Working with disadvantaged youth
        1. who are the disadvantaged
        2. sub-culture groups
        3. what disadvantaged children are like in school
        4. what disadvantaged children miss

      B. Important factors when working with disadvantaged youth
        1. intelligence and testing
          a. verbal-linguistic limitations

    2. language—in the school setting
    3. girl-oriented schools
    4. concept of time—influence on behavior and learning

  C. The culturally deprived and their interest in education
    1. meaning of education
    2. education vs. the school

III. The Teacher Aide and Prescriptive Teaching: Past, Present, and Future

  A. Teaching—the same process for all
    1. who went to school
    2. how long they stayed
    3. how successful the program was in meeting its objectives

  B. Teaching at the beginning of the prescriptive era, now
    1. what the teacher is trying to accomplish
    2. how teaching methods differ from the past
    3. why a new method

  C. Teaching in the future
    1. some hypotheses on how the teaching process will change
    2. some new goals for teaching
    3. the use of 'hardware' and 'software' in teaching

IV. The Teacher Aide and Students' Attitudes

  A. Definitions of attitudes
    1. are emotionalized
    2. influence behavior
    3. resist change

  B. The development of attitudes
    1. normal and abnormal
    2. in the home
    3. out of the home

  C. The role of the school for attitudinal change and/or development
    1. identification of attitudes and their basis or lack thereof
    2. techniques for change

This lesson is appropriate for either a pre-service or in-service program of preparation for teacher aides. It may be included with good results within the organization of preparation programs directed and executed by higher education personnel whether on campus or in the local school district. The time requirements are: four thirty-minute periods in succession; one forty-five minute period following a 'break'; and one forty-five minute period at the conclusion of the lesson.

This lesson is adapted easily to the team teaching method. Each member of the team can make a presentation supported with visual and audio aids;— there are many available. The large group may then be divided into four smaller discussion groups according to each of the topics included in the lesson. A final session with all members of the instructional team serving as a panel for the whole class serves as a profitable reinforcement for the discussion groups.

A Summary Statement

The lesson outlines are meant to be the skeletal frame on which the body of each lesson can be shaped. It is the function of the director of any preparation program which may include a number of these outlines to choose instructors who will shape the body of each lesson to meet the particular objectives of that program. Relevance is the key word here. The shape of the lesson body and its relevance for those being prepared depend upon the following: a) the location, city-suburb-rural; b) the level of education the trainees bring to the classes; c) the level of competence desired by the institution(s) for which the teacher aides are being prepared to serve; and d) the personal bias and expertise of the instructors.

The rationale preceding each lesson contains clues to lesson development. These rationales were a synthesis of reasons for including each of the lessons in a number of preparation programs in which the authors were involved at the instruction, direction or developmental levels. The rationale for including any one of these lessons in a particular program of preparation may logically differ from that offered here. Those who find these lessons a useful starting point for planning their own preparation program are urged to take note of the non-task-oriented functions of teacher aides discussed in chapter II. These functions, when important to a school district, serve as a 'blanket rationale' for all lessons outlined above.

The comments following each outline will serve as a general organizational guide in developing your own preparation program. The techniques described are only those that have proven effective in several past preparation programs. The repeated suggestions to employ teaching techniques that force teacher aides to get involved with the lesson cannot be over-emphasized. Role-playing, demonstrations, laboratory sessions, extensive use of audio-visual materials and equipment, and interaction among the teacher aides, teachers and instructors have proven effective. The lecture method of presentation used in isolation is relatively ineffective in achieving lasting results. Comments on evaluation are included in Chapter IV. Suffice it to say here that repeated evaluations of the lessons included in this chapter are the basis for these remarks regarding the commentary on technique and organization following each outline.

Teacher aides in most systems represent a cross-section of the racial and ethnic groups in the school community served. In the picture below a group of aides are enjoying a social moment during an in-service training period. One notices in the picture the mixture of not only racial groups but also that of age groups.

It is most important that teacher aides have such moments as pictured. A fifteen minute recess for refreshments enhances a workshop in many ways. First, it is recognized that a brief interlude between learning activities improves one's ability to concentrate and therefore retain. Second, many aides may work in the same system or building and never have an opportunity to face common problems and perhaps solutions to those problems which would otherwise be forever hidden. Third, participating in a social period such as represented in the picture will provide many aides experiences which can later be applied—when they are called upon to assist with social activities associated with the classroom, e.g., when parents are invited as guests for culminating activities, parent's night, or similar situations.

CHAPTER IV

ASSIGNMENT OF TEACHER AIDES

The assignment of teacher aides to a particular building, office, instructional support unit, or classroom requires some unique considerations. To begin with there is an element of service to the community and the children in school closely related to that of supererogation; whether the program is voluntary or the aides are paid. Most aides do not need to work for money, and those who do need to be paid could earn considerably more working outside the school. This element of service to the school and community may cause administrators and teachers to show a bit more consideration for the preferences of the teacher aide regarding her assignment.

Another unique consideration with regard to teacher aide assignment is that, unlike all other school personnel, few aides begin service with specific tasks. They bring to the school skills and experience to be sure, but the environment of the school, children, faculty, and staff is somewhat unique in and of itself.

The disparity of ages, experience and formal education among teacher aides at the time of entering service to the schools is greater than that of any other category of persons working in the schools. This unique characteristic presents both advantages and disadvantages related to the assignment of teacher aides.

The above considerations in the assignment of teacher aides are the basis for the point of view expressed herein.

ASSIGNMENT OF TEACHER AIDES

A Joint Responsibility

It was suggested in Chapter II, that administrators and teachers share in the selection of teacher aides. It would naturally follow that after the teacher aides have been selected, the administrators and teachers should cooperatively arrive at decisions regarding assignments.

The administrator's role is that of fulfilling delegated responsibility and exercising authority delegated for the supervision and evaluation of all personnel within his building. Even though he must share the responsibility for the assignment of teacher aides with teachers who may be much closer to the functional level of the aides, the building administrator shoulders the ultimate responsibility and is held accountable. Professionally, the administrators' goals are the same as those of the teachers: he desires teacher aides to be of maximum service in terms of student learning. The administrator fulfills his responsibility for assignment by seeking the best information available from the new teacher aide and from his teachers relative to the educational objectives for which aides serve and the eventual evaluation of same.

Teachers, whom aides serve, must justify the addition of personnel as they do the purchase of equipment or supplies; — in terms of facilitation of instruction and learning. These are central to the teacher's task. Teachers are helpful in selecting teacher aides, and therefore their viewpoint regarding assignment of teacher aides should be of value. The proximity of the central focus of the school — teaching and learning — gives the teacher a vantage point from which to consider teacher aide assignment not enjoyed by the administrator. The teacher's responsibility for the assignment of teacher aides is primarily one of making all meaningful information available to the administrator. Secondarily, the teacher is professionally obligated to make the administrator's decision regarding assignment a correct one.

Flexibility — Key to Success

The ideal which the building administrators and teachers strive to attain in assigning teacher aides is: maximum benefit to all teachers and students, and full utilization of the aides' talent and experience. In order to achieve this goal, many organizational patterns have been tried. There isn't one best organization of teacher aides. What works well in one school may be ineffective in another, and the manner in which aides are organized for service within the building this year may be quite ineffectual next year.

Teacher aides assigned to the library or instructional materials center are of service to all the teachers and children served by these facilities. Often more than one aide is needed when the instructional materials center, including audio-visual equipment, is housed within the library. One aide may schedule equipment usage and operate the projectors in the rooms for teachers. Another may process teacher requests that have been approved, order materials (films), and catalog new equipment. Some teacher aides who serve in the library have had experience in other than school libraries. They make excellent assistants for the librarian, and even though not certified as a school librarian are helpful to both teachers and pupils.

The above two examples serve to illustrate the assignment of teacher aides to positions in which they serve many teachers or pupils. One more such example might be the clerical 'pool' where the aide assists in the office and, teachers may then send duplicating, an occasional letter to be typed, or other clerical chores to the office 'pool' for processing or expeditious completion.

Of a more limited sharing of service is an organization whereby one or two aides rotate their time and energy among several rooms of early or later elementary children; perhaps spending one half day during each two school days devoted to each teacher and her class.

The greatest incidence of one teacher aide assigned to one teacher is found among special teachers—notably those who teach the educable retarded. Teachers who use a lot of equipment for instruction such as art teachers, physical education teachers, and industrial arts teachers fare next best. The early elementary grades, K through 3, would be more likely to have a one teacher - one teacher aide arrangement than would high school history or general mathematics classes.

The assignment of teacher aides should be made on the basis of need, benefit to children and efficiency. Unfortunately, funding from outside the local school district is often available for paying teacher aides to serve in the number two or number three priority to the exclusion of equal or more important service positions. Administrators and teachers must cooperate to rectify inequality of teacher aide assignment. This can best be managed by maintaining a flexible assignment policy.

Growth = Change and Change = Growth

As aides learn while serving, and through preparation programs, they develop competencies that can accommodate changes in instructional method, the organization of the instructional program, and their own assignments. An experienced teacher aide with appropriate skills may be of invaluable assistance in a team teaching situation. In schools where teacher aides have been depended upon for more than a year, a change from a self-contained classroom organization in later elementary to a quasi-departmentalized organization may be more easily accommodated;—or vice versa—whichever is appropriate for maximum instructional benefit to the pupils. Greater flexibility of the instructional program, both organization and methodology, is enhanced when the support and service personnel (including teacher aides) of the school gain new competencies.

The schools, the teachers, and their students are continuously reacting to the presses of the society that maintains them. The development of a technological world, the knowledge explosion and communications improvement have all exacted new demands for excellence in education. Some of the notable reactions—changes—in education have been increased emphasis on individualized instruction, increased use of machines, and more efficient means of exposing students to an ever increasing amount of information. The development of the controlled reader, the 8mm single concept loop film and projector, language laboratories, taped television instruction, computer-assisted instruction and programmed texts has been relatively recent in education. These changes and more to come demand growth by all who would serve in the schools. Teacher aides, who themselves only recently became a significant part of the education team, will find their very survival as service and support assistants depends upon their continual professional growth.

Evaluation

The evaluation of teacher aide services within a school system or a particular building in a school system should be carried out at two levels. One, an evaluation of the program as a whole by an administrator-teacher team; and two, the evaluation of individual teacher aide task performance by a teacher-administrator team. These two parts of the total evaluation should be semi-annual.

The criteria for evaluation of any educational endeavor must include the goals and objectives set forth when said educational endeavor was initiated. The primary goals of a program of service and assistance are: to allow teachers more time for individualized instruction, to make possible the incorporation of new equipment and materials into the instructional program; and to make additional resources and personal communications with the community available to the student. The specific task performances by teacher aides are secondary objectives by which the primary goals may be achieved. The most reliable evaluations of teacher aide programs are planned in advance, carried on continuously, communicated to all concerned—especially those persons being evaluated—; and culminated in a written report.

The question often asked regarding the evaluation of teacher aide programs, especially those included in Title I projects, is, "Why have an evaluation?" "We know whether our aides are giving good service." The truth is—most school officials really don't know with any degree of certainty. This leads to slipshod or poorly planned changes in the instructional program. Or worse yet, no change whatsoever. A well conceived and appropriately executed evaluation of teacher aide services is of value to the administrators, teachers and students because the information contained in the written report is a basis for decision-making.

First, the evaluation report may support decisions regarding methods of instruction to be employed by teachers. Second, it may be essential for decisions regarding curriculum. Third, organizational decisions that may inhibit or facilitate curriculum change or development and the instructional methods used, may rely on the evaluation. Finally, there should be some basis for decisions regarding individual teacher aide reassignment, retention or release. These decisions relating to members of the community—teacher aides—should be exemplary of the thoroughly fair manner in which the school administrators arrive at decisions.

Many school districts employ an outside consultant to plan, conduct and report in writing their evaluation of the teacher aide program of service. When in-service preparation programs are an integral part of the overall teacher aide program in the school, it is usual to include a separate evaluation of the in-service preparation program. Your authors have conducted many evaluations such as these, and believe the importance of the written report to subsequent decision-making to be of great value. There is ample talent within most schools to carry out a worthwhile evaluation of the program of teacher aide service. The employment of outside consultants is merely a matter of expediency.

Some Concluding Remarks

The value of teacher aide service in schools has already been established in our nation's schools. At long last teachers are free to teach—relieved of money collecting, lunch room supervision, equipment management and similar chores. The promise of new teaching techniques, innovative instructional organizations, and the new hardware and software of programmed or computerized instruction can be reality if the teachers have adequate assistance. At this writing no educator has seriously suggested machines serve *as*

79

ASSIGNMENT OF TEACHER AIDES

teachers. But if the machines are to serve teachers in the instruction of youth, then it is imperative that teachers have assistance. The master teacher must plan every moment of instruction and use every available device or method reasonable if today's youth are to survive in tomorrow's ever more complex society. The vast majority of teacher aides helping the teacher in this endeavor are justifiably proud to be of service.

It can be said with certainty that teacher aides entering the schools in 1975, will find that only the names are the same—teachers, student, instruction and learning—the rules of the game and its pace will be different. To be of maximum effectiveness in this service to schools and the children enrolled, teacher aides must continue to learn, to prepare themselves intellectually, and to re-train themselves for new tasks as they develop. This is most efficiently accomplished through preparation programs developed especially for teacher aides. School officials, teachers, parents and administrators must make every effort to facilitate programs of preparation for teacher aides.

The effort and expense necessary to incorporate teacher aide programs of service and to provide these aides with preparation or re-training does result in additional hours of instruction, additional minutes of individual attention to students, and increased use of instructional materials and equipment. The children reap a bountiful harvest of educational benefits.